*The precepts of Freefall Writing provide a foundational practice for any writer, but I'm convinced that the way Barbara talks about writing is an even greater source of learning.*

— Geoff Mead, PhD, Visiting Fellow, Saïd Business School, University of Oxford, UK

*...at each stage of my Freefall learning I have unfailingly received what I needed—I have been shown which sentences engaged the reader, and why some did not; I have had my intentions understood and enjoyed, and I have been given new ways of taking the writing further that were within my grasp.*

— Judith Hemming, Constellations Therapist, UK

*Barbara revealed that writing really involves both the act of putting forth the words, and the act receiving of them. How I receive other people's writing, how I ruminate and respond, requires the same faculties and skills that I require as a writer.*

— Kaye Gersch, PhD, Psychoanalytic Psychotherapist, Australia

*For the last two years, Barbara's fortnightly feed-back on my writing has dropped like a jewel into my inbox...there is an impatience to each of those jewels in my inbox, an urgent and stirring reminder to tap into, trust, and write from the raw energy of nascent insight—one lying beyond surface memory or fantasy that I never thought I would find.*

— Rebecca Ellis, UK

*Barbara Turner-Vesselago showed me a sort of struc-tureless structure that allowed an expansion of what I'd been doing in my fishing essays. Suspend judgment, trust the process and, most importantly, keep writing.*

— Tom Ohaus, US

*My writing group, following Barbara Turner-Vesselago's discoveries, outlined in* How to Talk About Writing, *'divine' together—both in our writing and in the talk that follows...Feedback from the group merges with the writing. We colour in the moments when each person's words filled our beings, enjoy story specific dialogue and see the wisdom of not tinkering. Smiles spontaneously erupt, and 'aha' gasps fill the room as insights ignite and are absorbed.*

— Georgina Mavor, Psychologist, Australia

# How To Talk About Writing

## A Fundamental Shift in Perspective

**BARBARA TURNER-VESSELAGO**

ISBN: 978-1-925846-72-0 (paperback edition)
Published by Vivid Publishing
A division of Fontaine Publishing Group
P.O. Box 948, Fremantle
Western Australia 6959
www.vividpublishing.com.au

A catalogue record for this
book is available from the
NATIONAL LIBRARY OF AUSTRALIA    National Library of Australia

# **CONTENTS**

# Foreword

This splendid guide lights the way for all of us who long to give helpful feedback to writers asking for our input, but who don't always know how or where to begin.

As a writing teacher, editor and publishing consultant whose mentoring approach has been transformed by the principles that Barbara Turner-Vesselago outlines in this book, I can vouch for the power of moving away from old paradigms of criticism and toward giving feedback that is sincere, perceptive and honours another's creative journey.

Facilitating community writing workshops for over six years in a small town on the south coast of Western Australia, I witnessed the profound effect of creating a culture around writing founded (as is recommended here) on encouragement and respect. Some of my students had no prior experience in creative writing. A few were barely literate, while others had decades of experience as professional writers. And yet many of them kept returning to my classes and telling me that for the first time in years, or ever, they felt inspired and hopeful about their writing.

One of my students used to sit through my classes with tears trickling down her cheeks. At first I worried, thinking I'd said something to upset her. But when I spoke to her privately after class, I discovered her tears were not of sadness but of homecoming: of finding a safe place in which she could express and explore her creativity and her life stories without fear of inappropriate judgment. Another student, with a long and accomplished background in journalism, once wrote that my workshops had "opened fresh summer breezes onto wintry landscapes" and helped her bid farewell to "the strictures of the sub-editorial craft."

I believe I was able to create these safe spaces for other writers to grow and blossom because of what I had learned from my longtime mentor, Barbara Turner-Vesselago: the power of focusing on what works and of having faith that each of us, with the right kind of feedback, can find and nurture an original writing voice that flows freely from within.

As a child, I loved to write. Stories poured out of me like bees from a hive, buzzing with life and color. But along the way, like so many, I received the wrong kind of feedback. I remember, in high school as a thirteen-year-old, receiving back an angst-filled short story covered in my English teacher's red pen.

Words and sentences were scratched out in red biro with scrawled admonitions like "too melodramatic!", "implausible", "cliché" and "excessive". As the story was the result of a genuine desire to write creatively and authentically, these words seemed not only to damn my dream of being a published author one day, but also to label me as someone with problems who needed help.

After that experience the bees retreated and the hive of endless story-honey fell dormant, a dried-out husk from which I could only occasionally draw a tiny trickle of inspiration. I reigned in my 'excessiveness' and focused instead on developing the analytical and essay-writing skills that were expected, praised and rewarded by teachers and parents.

The longing remained: to be a writer, to tell stories, to fly from one flower of experience to another, gathering pollen and making honey. But my wings wouldn't carry me anymore, and I couldn't find the hive that would help me turn moments of creative vision into honey.

And then, in 1994, in my late twenties, I attended a weekend workshop with Barbara Turner-Vesselago at the University of Western Australia. Her simple 'Freefall Writing' precepts allowed me to step back into the creative flow that had been blocked for so long, and her feedback gave me faith that my journey of words and stories was one worth continuing.

I discovered a writing voice I could trust and a garden of possible stories to share. Flower by flower, I would find my way home.

Over the decades, I have attended many of Barbara's 'Freefall Writing' workshops—each retreat an opportunity to explore new writing territory unhindered. But as much as enjoying a safe space to write, I have cherished them as a supportive space in which to talk about writing—my own and others'.

Not only has Barbara travelled the traditional path of higher education, to earn a PhD in Literature at the University of Cambridge, but she has also mentored hundreds of beginning and experienced writers, through her unique 'Freefall Writing' method, to develop their authentic writing voices in stories and memoirs uniquely their own. Many of her students have been published to wide acclaim.

With the insight and simplicity that can only come from decades of practice, Barbara has distilled the essentials of her teaching approach into six discoveries that will assist even the most seasoned writing mentor or editor to fly free from the cage of conventional feedback and literary criticism. Others just venturing into the world of writing discussion groups or taking on the role of a 'beta-reader' to give feedback on unpublished stories, novels and memoirs, will find straightforward guidelines—easy to comprehend and instantly rewarding to apply.

Following these guidelines, we can help writers find the best way forward to whatever they need to accomplish in their writing for now—whether their purpose be personal reflection and meaning-making, connecting more intimately with others through shared stories, or creating a finished work for publication.

Barbara Turner-Vesselago offers a fundamental shift in perspective that will help all readers find a beneficial and compassionate relationship to the writing they are asked to consider. Giving useful feedback is a matter of discovering what works—and here to guide us, at last, is someone who can talk about this journey with wisdom and clarity.

May all who read this little book be empowered to find and nurture the original writing voice that flows freely from within—whether in their own or in another's writing.

Let the revolution begin!

*– Nicola-Jane le Breton*

# We Need to Know How to Talk About Writing

Until just a few decades ago, writing was considered to be a solitary activity. "I didn't know he/she was a writer!" friends might exclaim when someone's first book was published. Writers laboured away, often in secret, asking only the opinion of a cherished friend or mentor—if anyone—before sending their work out to a publisher.

But since the middle of the last century, the value writers place on sharing their work-in-progress has changed dramatically. Writers' groups, writing seminars, and online writing forums are flourishing, and almost no-one publishes a book, or even finishes a first draft, without having shown it to other people in its earlier stages. As a result, nearly everyone who writes or who knows someone who writes is going to be called upon, sooner or later, to talk about writing.

> *...nearly everyone who writes or who knows someone who writes is going to be called upon, sooner or later, to talk about writing.*

Unfortunately, our understanding of how to talk about writing— of what it is most helpful for writers to hear about their writing—has not kept pace with this escalating trend.

Most writing group discussions, like most writing seminars, are free-for-all sessions where everyone tells the writer whatever occurs to them, from comments about sentence-length and word choice, to reminiscences about their own experiences, to judgments about what, in their opinion, this piece of writing should be or where it should go. And if the writing is conspicuously autobiographical, the problem is compounded. "That's not what really happened," someone may say, or, "How brave of you to write that!" or even, "Have you thought about going into therapy?"

Having devoted considerable effort over the years to picking up the pieces for writers who have received feedback that was *not* helpful, I have come to regard such free-ranging discussions as a kind of bloodbath—a Roman gladiator show, where some writers are killed off permanently, some are maimed, and almost no-one escapes unscathed. Yet many writers think they ought to be rugged enough to withstand these sessions. "Tell me anything," they announce, drawing themselves up into their best 'be strong' persona. "No, no, no," I want to say. "That is absolutely *not* what your writing needs. You don't want to hear 'anything' anyone wants to tell you. *You want to hear what's going to help the writing.*"

We all want to help when we talk about writing. We don't set out to discourage people, or to drive their creative impulse into hiding. We may feel compelled to uphold certain 'standards' in writing. But as I see it, that's just one face of a deeper intention: to help each person's writing become the best it can be. By taking time to think in advance about how it is most helpful to talk about writing, we become able both to stimulate the writing and to uphold what we consider to be the standards of the craft.

To speed that process along, I would like to share with you the six most crucial discoveries I've come to over the years regarding how best to talk about writing—discoveries that have helped numerous manuscripts find their way from their earliest glimmerings in 'Freefall Writing'[1] to acclaim as fully realized publications.

# The Six Discoveries

## 1. Silence Is Not Golden

I came into writing from academia and arts journalism (including book reviewing), so I was already pretty confident when it came to giving feedback about writing (even though there were many things I had to unlearn, to make that feedback useful to writers). But I've come to understand that for many people, the confidence to respond to a piece of writing is harder to come by. In most of the groups I've led, one or two people sit stony-faced throughout the discussion and say nothing at all. "Why don't they say something?" I used to wonder "Why are they being so withholding?"

I now know, from probing further, that the problem is not that they don't respond internally to the writing, or that they think it's beneath their notice. They may, in fact, think it's wonderful. But they don't know what to say. They may think other people in the group are making articulate, insightful comments, and wonder what they could say that would measure up. Or they may believe there's one right way to approach this piece of writing, but they don't yet know what that is. If they wait a little longer, their thinking goes, it will all become clear.

Alas, I don't know of a single writer who doesn't interpret silence in response to their writing as negative. Perhaps all writers are by definition insecure. Writing comes from a place so far beyond the everyday, conscious control of the ego that it can be difficult to reel it back in again. This means that the relationship between the writing and the ego is shaky at best. Most writers need some reassurance.

> *I don't know of a single writer who doesn't interpret silence in response to their writing as negative.*

It doesn't take much to satisfy the part that needs reassurance. "I really enjoyed this," works fine. Or, "I felt very moved by this piece of writing." I knew one novelist who had programmed her husband, when she showed him what she'd written each day, to say, "I love that. Keep going." And even though she'd set up this response in advance, it seemed to be enough to do the trick.

You can go on to be more specific about what in the writing made you feel that way, and even to talk about what you think could be improved (when the time is right to do this—a consideration I'll expand on later). But even if you're not sure what worked for you, a simple state-ment about how you're feeling now that you've read (or heard) the piece will lift the writer's suspicion that you hated it. *Silence is not golden.* Just say something, please.

## 2. Give Energy to What's Working

Over time I've learned that what I don't pay attention to in people's writing—especially when that writing is in its earliest stages—falls away in due course, whereas what I do pay attention to, increases. It's a discovery I recognize from numerous spiritual teachings: "That to which you give energy grows in your life." So I put my attention on articulating what works well for me in a piece of writing, and on conveying this to the writer. I purposely don't focus on whatever isn't working for me (although if a problem persists, I will find a way to address it at a later stage in the development of the piece).

It seems to be easier for most of us to identify what we don't like in someone's writing than to perceive and talk about what we do like. My guess is that this has to do with how we—and our parents—have been educated. Even when writing is in its earliest stages, its faults can seem to leap out from the page. "Surely I get to talk about this," goes the inner monologue, "Surely they need to know this." When these messages are the loudest ones you hear, it's worth asking yourself, "What kind of atmosphere would I like to write in? How would I like to feel, in order to write at all?"

> *Me, I like to feel encouraged, and as if I have something to offer. So why would I not want to foster that feeling in another writer?*

Me, I like to feel encouraged, and as if I have something to offer. So why would I not want to foster that feeling in another writer? Why would I not try to identify what they, uniquely, bring to the table? What do I *like* about this piece of writing?

As simple as it looks now, getting to this point required a huge shift in my way of responding. I was hell-bent, in my early teaching days, on pointing out whatever I thought was amiss with students' writing. I honestly thought that was what I was there for. I can pinpoint the day—in fact, the moment—when this changed, although I still don't know exactly *why* it happened.

To support myself while I wrote my doctoral thesis, I taught various courses in the English department of a large technical college. And I hated it. No-one, of course, signs on at a 'tech' to improve their writing and language skills. English courses were mandatory, and the students were grudging and unresponsive. There was a lot about the way they wrote to criticize, so I did. I worked hard at highlighting what they were doing wrong and explaining what they should do about it.

When the mid-term results came out, one of my students marched up to me after class, scowling. He was a big man, and I shrank back against the blackboard as he stood over me, shouting. "I am excelling in all my other courses! But you are failing me in English!" he boomed. "Everything else! A-plus!" His fist pounded the blackboard. I stood there, listening to him pound and shout, and then something in me shifted. "I know," I found myself saying. "And that's why it's so exciting."

His fist froze in mid-air. "It *IS*?" I felt almost as astonished as he did, but I kept on going. "Yes, I think you're right on the edge of a breakthrough!" "I AM?" He looked absolutely stunned. I nodded. "That's right. Any day now, it's going to happen."

Before my eyes, he straightened up and seemed to settle down several sizes. He stared at me a little longer, and then he nodded once and turned away. From then on, he worked hard, and before long he had the breakthrough I was talking about.

Meanwhile, my approach to teaching changed completely. I began to focus on what people were doing right, rather than on what they were doing wrong, and the classes became fun for a change. At the start of the next semester, a group of students I had failed the previous year returned, and one of them said to me, "Your teaching style is unrecognizable. You're like a completely different person." I felt surprised and pleased, but a quiet voice inside me said, "I know." Wherever the knowledge had come from in me, I had finally learned the value of encouragement.[2]

But what about the problems I see in a piece of writing? Is it fair to the writer to ignore them while I talk about what I do like? Am I not short-changing someone who has specifically asked me for feedback?

The answer to that question depends entirely on the stage the writer has reached with that piece of writing. Is it their first pass? Have they revised it? How often? Different kinds of feedback become appropriate at different stages of the writing (see Discovery 3, below).

These days, with writing in its earliest stages, I hardly notice the problems, because I'm so focused on what for me is going well. If I do see some central problem with the piece, something with which I think the writer will continue to struggle, I might make a practical suggestion to fast-forward the process. But I do so more or less in passing, on the principle of "those who have ears, let them hear". I might say, for example, "I generally find that sticking to one point of view works best in a short story," trusting that if there is something useful in this information, they will recognize it, rather than feel criticized. Then I go back to talking about what interests me in the piece: whatever is working well for me.

In this way, I'm devoting most of my attention to what the writer has achieved in the piece, knowing this will influence what comes next. It's the best way I know to ensure that this writer's unique contribution to writing will continue to unfold. And after years of watching writers move from strength to strength under this kind of influence, I have every confidence that this will be the case.

## 3. Suit Your Comments to the Stage of the Writing

Some of the most damaging comments writers can hear about their writing aren't the least bit ill-intentioned. They're just inappropriate. There's a mismatch between the stage the writer has reached with a piece of writing and the nature of the comment being made about it.

Most of us base our understanding of what good writing is, and how it works, on published work we've read. But typically, when we are asked to talk about someone's writing, it's a work-in-progress. This story, or memoir, or poem is so far from being fixed in its trajectory that a comment that would be perfectly appropriate at a later stage can throw it right off-track now, in ways the person commenting would never have intended.

*One of the most helpful things we can do when we talk about writing is to bear in mind the stage it has reached, and what sort of comment might be useful right now.*

One of the most helpful things we can do when we talk about writing is to bear in mind the stage it has reached, and what sort of comment might be useful right now. What can we offer at each stage that will both reflect what we're hearing[3] in the writing and help the writer to continue?

### i. The Early Stage

Much of the writing I'm asked to read is in its earliest stages, when the creative process is typically at its most wild and free. This is the time when the writer needs to pay attention to impulses and possibilities that were, up to now, inchoate. When I give feedback about work this new, I want to be able to reach into the very heart of it—into the connection between the writer's inspiration (what has energy for them) and what's coming out on the page. The last thing I want is for the writer to get attached to the surface of the work—to start focusing on the words they've used rather than on meeting the impulse that gave rise to them. It would be completely inappropriate to comment, for example, on sentence length or word choice—comments which will become useful at the much later, copy-editing stage.

I've found, with early-stage writing, that it's helpful to the writer for me to move through the pages as if I'm an infrared scanner, gauging my own energy as I go, and reflecting back to them what I find. Where am I most fully involved? Where do I feel less engaged? Are there moments when my mind wanders? Surprisingly often, this rising and falling of my energy or engagement as I read mirrors the writer's own. So the feedback I give at this stage reflects those shifts, focusing as always on where I am engaged, rather than where I'm not: "There's energy for me here, and particularly here." (It's important to include the phrase "for me", to emphasize that this is a subjective process and my comments don't reflect an absolute truth.)

Emotion is also an excellent source of feedback at this stage of the writing. If I'm moved by the writing, I don't try to hide it. I'll never forget the first time I realized someone had been moved to tears by something I'd written. It felt impossible, electrifying. Nowadays, if a group has assembled to hear writing and give feedback (as in, say, a writing seminar), I consider it a real boon to the writer if there are participants who respond directly with their emotions rather than through their intellect. I know that a show of feeling will immediately cut through any doubts the writer may have about the impact of what they've written. A response like this is remarkably effective in letting someone know how their work is coming across.

## ii. The Middle Stage

The next stage in the development of someone's writing is more challenging to respond to appropriately. Here, typically, the writer is still creating new material, but has begun to bring some intention into the mix. They've identified the core or essence of the piece, even if only half-consciously, and that central focus is now drawing new material to it, as well as helping them to refine what they've already written. So it's a mixed stage of inspiration and intention, where an ill-timed comment or piece of advice can still throw the writer off-track.

When you're asked to talk about writing that seems to fall into this middle stage—when, say, the writer has declared their intention for it to be a memoir piece or a short story—just reflecting back what has energy for you, or how the work made you feel, may not be as useful as it was before. But I don't find it helps right now to give a writer feedback about their structural or stylistic choices, either. This is still a work-in-process, and what is most essential to it may not yet be on the page.

At this stage, the writers I work with seem to find two things beneficial. The first is to hear what their readers/listeners think their work might be about. And the second is to receive answers to specific questions that they, the writers, already find themselves asking about their work.

Some time ago, a young writer-friend in British Columbia told me about a university writing seminar she had taken in the Okanagan, led by American-Canadian novelist, Jane Rule. "When we had all read someone's writing," she said, "we went around the circle, and each of us said what we thought it was about. And that was all we did." She went on to say, "The writer didn't respond; they just sat there and took it in."

When I heard this, I thought, "Brilliant!" At this middle stage, which is the stage most writing has reached by the time it hits a university seminar, the work may have been shaped, but it's still not ready to withstand a free-ranging critique. What Rule devised is a highly structured way of responding, and also—perhaps equally important—of *limiting* the response. It uses the presence of a group of people to help the writer find out whether or not their nascent intention for the piece—their sense of what draws it together—is what's actually being conveyed. Feedback about this issue from one person would be useful at this stage. From several people, it could prove to be invaluable.

Notice that Rule was not suggesting they ask the writer, "What is this about?" (a question that can throw the largely non-intellectual process of creation into a tailspin). Nor was she inviting suggestions as to what it *should* be about, which can be dangerously distracting for a writer to consider at this stage. To hear from several people what *they think* it's about, while in no way invasive, offers useful information which would be hard for the writer to find out any other way. So I suggest you ask a writer whose work strikes you as being at this middle stage, "Would you like to know what I think it's about?" Make it clear that you are not inviting the writer to discuss your opinion with you, which would benefit no-one. But see if they believe that hearing it will help them right now with their work-in-progress.

The other big opportunity writers can seize at this stage is to ask the questions that arose for them as they wrote. General questions directed at readers/listeners, like, "Is this any good?" or "What else do you need?" are not going to yield useful answers, because whatever the writer may hope the piece will become is not yet fully on the page. But if they've been wondering, for instance, if it gets boring around page 3, or if anyone understands what they were trying to do on page 5, now is an excellent time to seek specifics about readers' responses.

I strongly suggest writers pose these questions *before* they provide the manuscript, so readers can keep them in mind as they listen or read. And I also suggest they limit people's feedback *to* those questions, and direct the discussion back to them, each time it threatens to wander off-topic (as it will). That way they can sidestep any well-intentioned but (at this stage) potentially hazardous advice that some readers or listeners may feel an irresistible impulse to give.

Confronted with a writer who hasn't asked for specific feedback (perhaps because they think they should be strong enough to hear anything their readers want to say), just ask, before you read their work, what their purpose was in giving it to you: "What, specifically, do you want to know?"

### iii. The Revision Stage

The most useful time for a writer to solicit wide-ranging feedback from selected readers or a 'critiquing group' comes when that writer has done all they can think of to do with a piece of writing. I have never forgotten the wisdom of novelist and children's writer Tim Wynne Jones's reply when I asked him if he thought critiquing groups were useful: "Sure, as long as you take them your eighth draft and tell them it's your first."

Jokingly, he was acknowledging both the danger of presenting work for general feedback too soon, and the value of receiving it when the time is right. When the choices a writer has made have become so (relatively) conscious that others can shine a spotlight on them without scaring the mice from the barn, that is the time for the breadth of discussion that occurs when a writer says, "Tell me anything".

When you're giving suggestions at this stage of the writing, remember to frame them as 'I-statements' (e.g. "I find the descriptive passage at the beginning too long") rather than as 'rules' about writing (e.g. "This is an example of the 'descriptive fallacy'") —for the simple reason that this is what such comments are. Any 'rules' about writing creatively (apart from basic grammar, which sooner or later a writer is going to have to pick up anyway) are just generalizations drawn from published writing. But presented as known facts—and some people typically want to show they're in possession of such 'facts'—these generalizations can both shut down the discussion of a piece of writing and (for me, more alarmingly) inhibit the writer's originality. I have seen many pieces of writing shift from startlingly original to boringly conventional, under pressure from 'rules' about writing delivered by members of a peer critiquing group.[4] Saying "I think" and "I find" removes the false air of authority from these statements and restores them to your own personal repertoire of responses and suggestions, where they belong.

I think it's wise, even at this stage, for the writer to maximize the usefulness of this opportunity by asking specific questions they have about the piece. And I think it's wise for readers to continue to emphasize what's working for them. But now is the time when people can most usefully comment on anything they think is relevant, even down to fine points of punctuation, or specific word choices (see also Discovery 4 below, 'Read As If You Wrote It'), still using qualifiers like "I think" or "in my view", of course. A writer who has reached this stage with a piece of writing will usually feel solid enough not to take comments on board if they don't feel relevant, and may well be able to hear advice of all sorts without being thrown off course.

### iv. Post-publication

By this stage, your work as a reader/listener is done. The writing you've been talking about is out in the great world, and there's nothing anyone can do about it. Beyond this, unless you're a reviewer or a critic, I think it's a mistake to give any feedback at all.

Early in my career as a literary mentor, at a dinner held by one of my students to celebrate the publication of her story in a high-profile literary magazine, champagne was poured, and the writer read out her story. But as I listened, I heard something in the opening, which was new, that felt contrived to me—something the magazine's editor had clearly encouraged her to add. So as the chorus of approval died down, I started to tell her what I felt was wrong with it.

In the deep chill that followed, I realized something I have borne in mind ever since: it is unwise to suggest improvements on something now fixed on the page by publication. For one thing, it's pointless. The story has gone out into the public domain and can't be drawn back again. It is what it is. Even more important, now is the time to celebrate the full arc of its achievement:

> *...it is unwise to suggest improvements on something now fixed on the page by publication.*

a series of steps, each one demanding work, which is now complete. The only job remaining to those who knew it as a work-in-progress is to raise their glass.

## 4. Read As If You Wrote It

Even at the critiquing stage, the most useful feedback you can give a writer often comes from reading their writing in a certain way. When you read the writing *as if you wrote it*, you can situate yourself beneath its surface and respond from an understanding of choices the writer has made, rather than just give your verdict on their outcome. In other words, you can move from judgment (which is often the first level of response) to deeper comprehension through the shared act of writing. At this level, what you have to say becomes truly helpful.

*When you read the writing as if you wrote it, you can situate yourself beneath its surface and respond from an understanding of choices the writer has made, rather than just give your verdict on their outcome.*

Here's an example. If someone writes of their heroine's new love-interest, "He had a twinkle in his eye," my first reaction might be: "Oh, what a cliché." If a few more clichés follow in short order, I may find myself wanting to offer that judgment to the writer: "You write in clichés." As a result, they'll feel ashamed or discouraged. They'll feel, when they write, more self-conscious, more vigilant, in the hope of preventing this from happening again.

But self-conscious and vigilant is the opposite of what a writer needs to be, in the writing state. It's infinitely preferable to be relaxed and receptive, fully absorbed in the world they're writing about. If I'm listening as if I wrote that piece, I can ask myself: "What do I do when I write a cliché like 'a twinkle in his eye'?" The answer is simple: I reach for a phrase that has worked before, something that I think most people will recognize, because doing so feels safer than risking an original one of my own. What I need to do, therefore, is to go deeper.

Now I'm onto something that may be useful to this writer. I can ask questions that will help the writer to move beyond that cliché: "What did that man's expression look like to you, when you said 'twinkle'?" or, "What did [your point of view character] actually see?"

You can use this technique of 'reading as if you wrote it' again and again, and it will continue to help the writing to progress. It also has a useful side-benefit for you, if you are a writer too. Because you have to keep asking yourself, "What am I really doing, when I write something like that?" you can't help but become more aware of choices you make in the act of writing, and why you make them. Increasingly self-aware (rather than self-conscious), you'll find yourself ever more capable of making the best choices that present themselves as you write, without interrupting the flow.

Even if you are not a writer, you can still use this technique to great advantage when you talk about writing.

Just ask yourself, "Why would I do [whatever it is you may feel critical of], if I were a writer?" The answer may not be hard to come by; it may be the sort of thing you do yourself in some other walk of life. (In the 'cliché' case, for example, you may repeat an old anecdote in conversation, rather than come up with a new one.) And once you have asked yourself why you do that, you are already at a deeper level where your response becomes useful, rather than painful, for the writer to hear about their work.

## 5. Know When You're Hooked and Take Care of That First

There is, however, one thing that will prevent you from reading or listening at that deeper level, and that is what I call being 'hooked' by something in the writing. How can you tell when you're hooked? See if what you're hearing or reading makes you feel angry or irritable. See if you find yourself thinking it shouldn't have been written, or you shouldn't have been asked to read it.

Of course, neither of these is true. People can pretty much write what they want to write, and if you've agreed to read it, then it's your job to offer some helpful feedback. But there you are, feeling angry and trapped by what you're reading or hearing. If you find yourself in that situation, what do you do?

First of all, it's important to accept that not everybody is going to like every kind of writing. I, for example, have very little tolerance for what I think of as 'poo-poo and pee-pee' stories—stories that give a central role to bathroom humour. I feel bored and disappointed by them at first, then I feel irritated, and I have trouble thinking of anything useful to say. Since I already know this about myself, when I'm asked to comment on work like that, the most helpful thing I can do is to tell the writer, as early as possible, "I'm just not good with this kind of writing," and suggest they look for someone who will enjoy it. Because this is, after all, my problem, not theirs. There are going to be other people out there who like stories like this—aren't there? This writer deserves to hear from them about their writing, not from me.

There are also far more subtle ways to be hooked by someone's writing—ways that are perhaps more difficult to own. The cue for me is feeling self-righteous or judgmental about the writing. When I can spot that tone in my response (rather than simply acting from it), I know I have work to do on myself to unhook whatever is bothering me before I can give this writing—and this writer—the consideration they deserve.

I remember years ago, in a university writing seminar I was leading, hearing a well-groomed young woman in a business suit read out a piece of writing in which her point of view character, "I", was taken on a date to a bar where badly dressed dancers lunged around like apes, displaying their dismal IQs and primitive emotions in their dance moves and making her feel as if she'd walked into a cage at the zoo. I knew the other students weren't going to like it. But I didn't try to interrupt the storm of criticism that followed. "Well, this is how people respond," I thought. "She needs to know this."

But I felt a little uneasy at the time, and when I'd had time to reflect on the situation, I felt ashamed of myself. Clearly, I was hooked by what she'd written. I made the judgment that her "I" was wrong to judge those people in the bar, and I felt self-righteous about my opinion. It's true I didn't criticize her work overtly, but my job as the leader was to shift the discussion away from judgment, and toward what worked for us in the piece. By remaining silent, I let her fellow-students do the dirty work for me.

These days, I hope I would recognize the situation more quickly and take care of it—talk to myself in a way that would help me climb down off my high horse. Having done this, I would be able once again to think about the writing 'as if I wrote it': "Okay, if I wanted to get that point of view across in a story, what would I do?"

"But people don't get to say this kind of thing in writing," some part of me might still object. Nuh uh. Unless what's being said in a piece of writing actually violates some code of ethics upheld by society at large, they do get to say it. And if I want my response to be helpful to that writer, I need to deal with my own feelings of judgment and accusation first. I need to respond as a fellow human being, with shortcomings of my own. Most of all, I need to be able to respond as if I wrote it.

(While I was writing this, I could hear my husband, downstairs, say something on the phone that I was hooked by. I walked downstairs talking to myself, trying to understand why I was so hooked, but still, when I got to where he was, I tore a strip off him. Giving myself more time would have been a good thing. It's no easy matter to pull these hooks out, and simply reacting can feel so much more satisfying—no matter how unhelpful it is—at the time.)

## 6. Treat Autobiographical Writing as Writing

When someone presents you with a piece of writing that strikes you as autobiographical, ask them what they want to know about it. My bet is that they'll ask you how it works *as writing*, and not as a historical record, or a means of catharsis, or a cry for help. You need to be able to separate the writing from the person writing it, and discuss it in ways that will help them to separate from it, too. In order to do this, some clear boundaries, such as the ones I have had to develop in my own work with autobiographical writing, are essential.

One of the most important of these is a boundary for the writer. For anyone to work with experiences from their own life, in writing, it's of enormous help if the material has time to settle—to 'compost', to use Natalie Goldberg's very apt term. For my students, I advise a ten-year hiatus, which seems enough time for most people to gain some distance from their subject matter. This length of time is usually sufficient for the writer's ego to have let go of what happened, and for the events themselves to have sent out shoots of connection and meaning, which emerge in the act of writing. The passage of this much time does nothing to affect the immediacy of the story. On the contrary, it allows the writer to narrate the story competently, while at the same time identifying in a lively way with its point of view character. Crucially for the discussion of the writing, it also enables most writers, most of the time, to listen to comments about the content of the work without taking them personally.

The other important boundary is for the reader. For me to help this writer find out how their piece works as writing, I must focus on treating it as writing, and not as any other thing (a personal sharing, a cry for help, etc.), just as I would a piece of fiction. In fact, I have no way of knowing for certain whether or how much of the work is autobiographical, even if it strikes me as being so. And if I can focus my response on the way the material comes across in writing, rather than on where I think it has come from, my feedback will become significantly more useful to the writer.

*... if I can focus my response on the way the material comes across in writing, rather than on where I think it has come from, my feedback will become significantly more useful to the writer.*

After one of my workshops in England, several of the participants formed a writing group, as they often do, this time with one slightly more experienced writer acting as facilitator. They carried on successfully for a while, according to the woman who told me this story. But then one day this woman, whom I'll call Angela, read out a piece of writing to which the facilitator responded, "Oh, poor Angela." "I couldn't write a word for weeks after that," she told me. When I asked her why she thought that comment had shut her down, she said, "I didn't want it to be about me. I wanted it to be something that can happen to a person." That is precisely why the writing must be treated *as writing*, rather than as something someone is telling us about themselves.

For such writing in its early stages, I talk about where the energy is for me, and where, as I read along, I feel most connected to it. At a later stage, when the writing is coming together as a coherent piece, I might discuss what I think it's about. And if it's been revised several times, I might give more technical feedback: what I think about the way it's structured, or the dialogue, the imagery, even the sentence structure—whatever strikes me as worthy of note in what's on the page. In other words, I try to treat autobiographical writing as I treat fiction.

One of the implications of this choice is that I don't get to say, "This is very courageous," even if the implicit act of writing this piece strikes me that way. To say that would be to draw a personal inference about the writer, and thus to make what literary critics call 'an illicit assumption'. Do I know this piece took courage to write? Perhaps the writer was in a witness state as they wrote it, one hundred percent present for what was going on in their mind, and not experiencing any particular feelings at all. I need to stay with the writing, and not stray into the territory of assuming anything about the writer.

Nor do I get to say, "I was there at the time, and that's not quite what happened." These characters and events are on the page now, and that page will work or not work as writing because of the choices the writer has made. Even if I know 'what really happened' myself, and would have told the story differently, my job right now is to focus on the work in front of me. If the events being recounted have been documented elsewhere, that, in my opinion, is a matter for this writer to take up further down the line, with their publisher, their publisher's lawyers, etc. If I am being asked to talk about how this page works for me as writing, that job does not include making a judgment as to whether this is an accurate or verifiable historical record.

I also don't get to assume that I can correctly identify the writer with any character in the writing, including a character who says "I". We all recognize that in fiction, an I-character can be anyone the writer wants her or him to be. But even if the writing sounds autobiographical, do we truly know that it is? Is the "I" in Shakespeare's sonnets—the one who declares his love for a man in one poem and a woman in another—Shakespeare himself? We will never know. For this reason, I try never to say "you" or "your mother" when I'm talking to a writer about their I-character or their I-character's mother. To separate that character from the writer in discussion by calling it "he" or "she" or "the I-character", rather than "you", just seems accurate to me. In addition, my feedback thus becomes less confronting to the writer, because it feels less personal. Immediately, it becomes easier to take in.

*The most scrupulously factual autobiographical writing is no longer simply a record of someone's personal history; it is a creation with purpose, with coherence, with drama and, the writer hopes, with significance for other people's lives.*

Even the material of real life, recounted in the so-called 'natural' chronological order in which it unfolded, must, like any other impulse for writing, "suffer a sea-change/into something rich and strange" in the act of writing. It will be transformed in such a way as to gain meaning beyond the individual life. The most scrupulously factual autobiographical writing is no longer simply a record of someone's personal history; it is a creation with purpose, with coherence, with drama and, the writer hopes, with significance for other people's lives. Let writers of autobiography be afforded the same privacy for the sources of their writing that you would unthinkingly give writers of fiction. Stay with the words on the page and the effect they have on you, knowing that talk about anything else, however well-intentioned, will only inhibit the writer.

# A Fundamental Shift in Perspective

All of the discoveries listed above are ones I have found truly helpful to writers who show me their work-in-progress. I hope they will prove useful for you, too. If you are new to talking about writing, or have trouble doing it, they may seem a lot to bear in mind while you listen to or read a piece of writing. But in fact, they're all the result of a fundamental shift in perspective that makes the whole enterprise of talking about writing look very different. Instead of judging, I try to put myself in a writer's shoes to see what would help me if I had written the piece, and at what stage it would help. Then I investigate what lies behind my judgments as a reader/listener, so I can trust my feelings and my engagement. It all begins with a desire to help, not harm, the writing (and the writer).

*It all begins with a desire to help, not harm, the writing (and the writer).*

What these six discoveries represent are underlying directions you can move in when you respond to writing, not goals to achieve before you respond at all. Knowing this, you can start small. You can tell the writer something about what you're feeling, about the impact their writing has on you, without knowing exactly why. You can take a step toward not being hooked. (In the example I gave of my response to my husband, I count just being aware of the fact that I *was* hooked as a plus.) Remembering to notice how your engagement changes as you read along allows you to build a foundation for communicating where there is energy for you in a piece of writing.

As you pursue these directions in your own responses, don't be intimidated by other people's feedback. Some of the most intelligent, authoritative-sounding comments may be the most damaging to a writer's work. As I know to my regret, the fact that someone sounds as if they know what they're talking about doesn't mean they're helping. A few heartfelt words from you about what you're feeling might mean more to a writer, and to the realization of their work, than any other feedback that comes their way.

It helps to remember that any 'rules' about writing creatively are only generalizations drawn from what other writers have done before. They are tools, not rules: shortcuts that, if they're needed, will be very, very easy for a writer to learn.[5] What can't be learned intellectually are the very qualities that will make a writer's work powerful and unique: authority, the power to move people, strength of voice, and an ability to write with grace. None of these can be addressed by 'rules', and no-one who tries to do so will be doing anything relevant.

If, with early-stage writing, you can stay with what is working for you and how it affects you, and then, in later stages, put yourself in the writer's shoes to consider what they're trying to achieve and speak from there, you'll be offering something of inestimable value to help that writer realize their work-in-progress. And surely that's what we all want to do, when we talk about writing.

# (Endnotes)

1 FreefallWriting™ is an immersive rather than prescriptive approach to writing, which I have developed and now facilitate in workshops worldwide. *Writing Without a Parachute: The Art of Freefall* (Jessica Kingsley Publishers/Hachette 2013), and *Freefall Into Fiction: Finding Form* (Jessica Kingsley Publishers/Hachette 2017) provide step-by-step guides to the sequential stages of this approach.

2 A further point that could be made about my insight at the blackboard is that in that moment, I made a shift from judging that man's work as a product to encouraging it as a process. And when I shifted, so did he: "I'm in a process," he realized. "So I can get better." This understanding—that it is far more effective to treat writing as a process than as a product—has informed both the way I teach writing and the way I talk about it, ever since.

Psychologist Alfred Adler drew an important distinction in this regard about the difference between praise and encouragement: that praise has to do with product; encouragement with process. More recently, Ichiro Kishimi and Fumitake Koga have discussed, in their Adlerian self-help book, *The Courage to Be Disliked*, the fact that praise belongs to top-down situations where one person assumes power over another, while encouragement presupposes equal relationships within a horizontal field. Sense the impact on yourself of hearing, "This passage is working well" (praise), versus, "I find this passage really works for me" (encouragement). In the first instance, the speaker is passing judgment on a product (from a position of superior knowledge), whereas in the second, the speaker is responding as an equal, encouraging what they like best about the work and would like to see continue. This latter fact may be one of the reasons why, as a writer, one often finds that praise is as likely as criticism to stop the creative process in its tracks.

3 I say "hearing" and "listening" because I prefer to hear writing-in-progress read aloud. But even when I'm reading it, I'm listening—to the tone and the cadence of the writing voice in the piece.

4 Perhaps the earliest book of 'rules' about fiction was Percy Lubbock's *The Craft of Fiction* (1921), in which he drew from Henry James's novels and prefaces a sort of casebook as to what a novel should be. Novelists E.M. Forster and Virginia Woolf were so incensed by the idea that they wrote *The Art of the Novel* and "On Re-Reading Novels", respectively, to oppose the whole notion of prescriptive rules for fiction. I find it instructive, almost 100 years later, to see whose work we remember. Ironically, some of those same 'rules' are still being trotted out today.

5 The best tool-books, in my view, are the 'quick and dirty' ones that simply make a list of such generalizations, like Jack M. Bickham's *The 38 Most Common Fiction Writing Mistakes*.

# Quick Discovery Guide

These days, almost everyone who writes shows their work-in-progress to other people before they send it out to publishers, in the hope of receiving helpful feedback. This relatively new stage in the creative process has left many of us wondering: what sort of feedback really helps? In this book, I share six important discoveries that have allowed me to shift from judging the work I am given (and justifying my judgments) to joining the writer as his or her creative partner in a shared attempt to make the work the best it can be.

1. **Silence is not golden**

    Even if I have no idea what to say at first, I take care to make some comment, right away, about something that works well for me in the writing. Even a statement about how I've connected with it ("I felt moved by this piece of writing," or, "I was really absorbed in this") seems to help out of all proportion to the information I'm imparting, probably because it dispels the writer's default assumption that silence implies a host of negative judgments withheld.

2. **Give energy to what's working**

   I've learned from experience to focus on whatever works best for me in what I'm reading, on the well-founded principle that whatever we give energy to will increase, while whatever is ignored will fall away—in part, at least, because neither of us is paying any attention to it.

3. **Suit the comment to the stage of the writing**

   A different order of comments becomes useful at each stage of the writing. Be sure to find out, before you comment, how much work the writer has done on this piece.

   a) With writing that is brand new and relatively unformed, I talk about what I particularly connect with—thus implying, perhaps, what I'd like to see more of.

   b) When the writing has been revised or "pulled together" to some extent, I also try to say what I think it's about.

   c) When a writer asks me to comment on a "finished" draft—and only then—I mention what I think could be improved, and why.

4. **Read as if you wrote it**

   Writer or not, I try to put myself in the writer's shoes when I consider what I see as problems in the writing. Why might I have done what they did? This situates me below the surface of the writing, ready to ask questions that may help solve the problem rather than judge its outcome.

5. **Know when you're hooked**

   When I feel judgmental, righteous, or angry as I read, that signals to me that I've been "hooked" by something in the writing. If I want to be able to "read it as if I wrote it", I first need to identify that hook and detach it before I go on to think any further about the writing.

6. **Treat autobiographical writing as writing**

   I try to approach autobiographical writing the same way I do fiction: to talk about how it works for me *as writing*. This means I limit my comments to what works best for me, at first, and then proceed according to whatever stages the manuscript reaches thereafter (as described in #3). In other words, I stay with the words on the page, and *eschew any inferences about where this writing might have come from, or why.*

With the help of these six discoveries, I've taken up a new position with regard to the writing I'm given. I assume that when someone shows me their work in progress, I'm being asked to share in its evolution rather than judge it. With this kind of informed support, what's truly original in the writing flourishes, and talking about writing becomes a rewarding contribution to the process of creating it.

# A Brief Introduction to Freefall Writing

FreefallWriting™ is an approach to writing that teaches people, very quickly, what I consider to be the essentials.

First, you don't sit around thinking about writing; you plunge in and write. And having started, you don't stop yourself. I don't mean that you write without stopping—it's not that—but rather that you learn to write without dividing yourself into the writer and the reader or critic. Your job is to write. To that end, you don't change anything. You learn to let it be, and then see what you've written somewhere down the line.

And once you've entered another world in your writing, you learn to stay there. Stop. Look around. Take in (and write down) all the sensuous details. Follow the energy that's there for you and see where it takes you. Stay with what's happening, no matter how intense it gets—instead of, say, wandering off to see what's in the fridge. In other words, you write, and let the writing teach you what you need to know.

Often, the material that first arises when you simply write what comes up for you is autobiographical. But if enough time has passed since those events took place, that material will be of as much use to you in learning the essential skills of writing as anything you could invent, and often more so. The important thing is that it is what arose for you. And from that point, everything you will need to learn about the art of writing follows.

I first introduced this way of writing in a fifty-page book entitled, *Freefall: Writing Without a Parachute*. Later, I delved into the precepts of this process in much more detail in *Writing Without a Parachute: The Art of Freefall* (Jessica Kingsley 2013), designed to work both as a reference book and as a 12-month course, with exercises. That book was followed by *Freefall Into Fiction: Finding Form* (Jessica Kingsley 2017), which shows how to undertake the transition from Freefall through to fiction and memoir. I also teach workshops in Freefall Writing, worldwide.

www.freefallwriting.com

# What Others Are Saying About Barbara Turner-Vesselago's Feedback

In 2009, I decided that I wanted to write a book about storytelling. I had already attended a number of Freefall Writing workshops and Barbara agreed to mentor me. I sent her a collection of papers and waited for her initial comments. She sent back a dozen pages of detailed feedback, identifying some elements that could be developed into chapters. Her parting shot was both salutary and encouraging: "I think there might be a good book in here somewhere if you want to do the work."

It was obvious that turning my manuscript into a book worth reading would take a lot of work. But I could see from Barbara's notes that she had read my writing— all of it—appreciatively, and that, in the midst of my muddle of words, she had found at least a glimmer of potential. "There are too many bad books in the world," I replied. "Let's go for it."

Over the next 18 months, draft chapters flew back and forth between us. I devoured her feedback: "Lovely. Can you drop even more deeply into this scene?" "You've found an edge of vulnerability here that is very engaging." "Listen to the cadence of this sentence." "Very moving. I wept as I read this account of you and your son." "This chapter is very informative, but does it belong in this book?" And so on. And so on.

*In passing, I learned a lot about technique, but more importantly, as well as bringing out the best in my writing, the quality of Barbara's attention affirmed my growing sense of myself as a writer. The result was Coming Home to Story, published in 2011, followed by more books in succeeding years: creative non-fiction; memoir; children's fiction; and poetry.*

*None of this would have happened without Barbara's inspirational teaching and mentoring. The precepts of Freefall Writing provide a foundational practice for any writer, but I'm convinced that the way Barbara talks about writing is an even greater source of learning.*

— Geoff Mead, PhD, Visiting Fellow,
Saïd Business School, University of Oxford, UK
(www.narrativeleadership.org)

*It's hard to get right the mixture of criticism and encouragement that a developing writer needs, and in the past, I have been put off by too much general praise or too much specific criticism that easily daunted or shamed me. But at each stage of my Freefall learning I have unfailingly received what I needed—I have been shown which sentences engaged the reader, and why some did not; I have had my intentions understood and enjoyed, and I have been given new ways of taking the writing further that were within my grasp.*

*This is a priceless gift. It is as if Barbara has been by my side, not judging but helping me take new steps. And even when I remain unable to master a skill, story after story, I am given new ways of seeing what I nevertheless have mastered and what it would take to let go of certain habits that get in the way. Over time I've absorbed this level of generous encouragement so that I can keep going even when there are blocks and times of discouragement.*

*Feedback in a Freefall Writing group is similarly structured to maintain the focus on the writing rather than the writer, and to focus on what can be enjoyed and then taken further. These kinds of conversations may look simple, but I have come to see that it takes a deep maturity and kindness to be able to provide them, reliably and over a long period of learning.*

— Judith Hemming, Constellations Therapist, UK
(www.movingconstellations.com)

*I have been attending Barbara Turner-Vesselago's Freefall Writing workshops for about 25 years. Initially, I had no idea what to expect, and I arrived at the first workshop with a dictionary! I soon came to realize that it was myself, with all my senses, that I would require to participate fully.*

*Barbara revealed that writing really involves both the act of putting forth the words, and the act receiving of them. How I receive other people's writing, how I ruminate and respond, requires the same faculties and skills that I require as a writer. So as a writer, I provide all the sensuous detail, and as a reader, I can appreciate and comment on the impact that sensuous detail has on me. Likewise, as a writer, I immerse myself in a scene and convey this in what I write; as a reader I comment on the way the writer involved me in that scene and note the memorable details.*

*Are they conveyed by unique turns of phrase, or startling descriptions? Had I never thought of that before? Or is it that they remind me of the colour and light in a passage of my own life? How did I get to feel the salt in the sea-breeze, when salt wasn't specifically mentioned? How are emotional details conveyed in any piece of writing? What emotion did I 'get'? Did another reader get the same emotion?*

*So many different elements contribute to a writer's style: vocabulary, rhythm, humour and much more. What particular use has this writer made of these elements? Which elements really work for me? What writerly skills enable me to sink gratefully into a new book, as I did when I began Miss Garnet's Angel, by Sally Vickers? What held me all the way to the end?*

— Kaye Gersch, PhD, Psychoanalytic Psychotherapist, Australia (www.kayegersch.com)

*For the last two years, Barbara's fortnightly feedback on my writing has dropped like a jewel into my inbox. I have had the privilege of one-to-one mentoring and of attending yearly Freefall retreats during which she always talks intimately, generously, but never saccharine sweetly, about our writing.*

*Prior to meeting Barbara, I was writing within the strictures of academic peer review culture. Armed with a sharply honed inner critic, my writing had become full of fear and had all but ground to a halt. While Barbara sensitively tailors her feedback to anyone's particular stage of writing, she has no time for self-limiting forms of judgment.*

*Indeed there is an impatience to each of those jewels in my inbox, an urgent and stirring reminder to tap into, trust, and write from the raw energy of nascent insight—one lying beyond surface memory or fantasy that I never thought I would find. There is more to this reminder than meets the eye: I have come to realize that at the heart of Barbara's generosity is a call to detach my 'self' from the process and the product of writing.*

*Writing has become not only about sidestepping my ferocious inner critic, but about enjoying what is revealed as I get out of my own way. What I had not anticipated in this creative partnership is that I would be invited not only to breathe more energy into the writing, but also into life itself.*

— Rebecca Ellis, UK (www.rebeccayoga.org.uk)

*Years ago, I wrote fishing columns and features for magazines. Some publications wanted nuts and bolts, where-to, how-to, when-to kind of stuff. I wrote it but found the process tedious with a product that fell short of memorable. Thankfully, the publisher of one boating magazine wanted essays on fishing that non-fishers would enjoy reading—fishing as a metaphor to life. At that time, fishing felt like my reason for being. Expanding that feeling in writing came naturally.*

*Decades later, the themes and ideas of those essays still live in me. The writing lacked craft, but the energy and ideas still shine through. I loved the process of writing without any idea of where each month's column was going until I wrote it.*

*Well into my writing career, a friend suggested a Freefall workshop in La Push, Washington. Despite powerful internal resistance (like, who the hell wants to be sequestered in a cabin on the rainy, dreary shores of the North Pacific), I went. In that week, Barbara Turner-Vesselago showed me a sort of structureless structure that allowed an expansion of what I'd been doing in my fishing essays. Suspend judgment, trust the process and, most importantly, keep writing.*

*Some people do best with outlines, knowing where the story is going. Some mystery writers even start with the end and work their way back. I don't do that, but when I write, something good happens—the unknown becomes known, the characters do and say things I never anticipated. It's not my process to think about it, then write about it. All the answers come with the writing and Freefall, when I venture there, keeps me writing.*

— Tom Ohaus, US (www.anglingunlimited.com)

*When I write, it is akin to 'divining for water'. I immerse myself into words I wish to appear on the page. Not words that drift around like pollen on a breeze, but real words that touch the ground, fill the nostrils, graze or caress the skin, paint my eyeballs, harmonize my ears and perhaps more importantly emerge out of nothingness, like starlit fireworks on a calm, clear night. Mesmerized, I am drawn to them.*

*My writing group, following Barbara Turner-Vesselago's discoveries, outlined in* How to Talk About Writing, *'divine' together—both in our writing and in the talk that follows. One by one we read our work out loud, our writing companions gifting their 'presence', listening and feeling for resonance with words and sentences that pour into the space. Themes and metaphors, present but unformed a moment ago, are voiced. Feedback from the group merges with the writing. We colour in the moments when each person's words filled our beings, enjoy story specific dialogue and see the wisdom of not tinkering. Smiles spontaneously erupt, and 'aha' gasps fill the room as insights ignite and are absorbed.*

*Guided by Barbara's 'discoveries', we are buoyed by the space of nothingness. It continues to feed our thoughts in conversation and personal reflection. Our stories have been written, told and shared. We leave our place of succor, expanded and open to the stories that await.*

— Georgina Mavor, Psychologist, Australia
(www.thereadingcoachoz.blogspot.com)

# Other Books by Barbara Turner-Vesselago

**Writing Without a Parachute: The Art of Freefall**

*This book has something most instruction completely misses: a practical set of exercises and explanations to help with the imaginative act of original composition.*

— Mimi Thebo, Senior Lecturer in Creative Writing,
Bath Spa University

*Read this book, whether you want to be a professional writer or more likely someone—basically all of us—who needs to find and hear your own voice and let it flow, so that your life will also flow.*

— Richard Moss, author of *The I That is We*
and *The Black Butterfly* (Celestial Arts)

**Freefall Into Fiction: Finding Form**

*Barbara maps the dangerous journey from intuitive 'Freefall' writing to consciously created fiction [and memoir], making it exhilarating: a lucid, well-researched and clearly illustrated guide we can safely follow.*

— Dr Gillie Bolton, author of *The Writer's Key: Introducing Creative Solutions for Life* and 11 other books on writing

*Barbara Turner-Vesselago guides us through the heart of the creative process, using experiential exercises and practical tips to enable the aspiring writer to develop a 'first draft' into a more expanded and refined piece of work. I have wanted to write for years...this book made me feel that I can't wait to start!*

— Debra Penman, co-author of *Writing Well: Creative Writing and Mental Health*

## YOUR PATHWAY TO SUCCESSFUL BOOK PUBLISHING

**Fontaine Publishing Group** is Australia's highest-rated publishing services provider.  We work with independent authors, small to large businesses and organisations to produce tailored publishing solutions that are appropriate, elegant and viable.

–  www.fontaine.com.au  –